Beliefs: A Children's Guide to Religion

BELIEFS

A CHILDREN'S GUIDE TO RELIGION

SVEN O MAG

Beliefs: A Children's Guide to Religion

Book design by Sven O Mag
Images courtesy of www.rgbstock.com:
Sigurd Decroos, Lynne Lancaster, Michael Lorenzo, Dez Pain

First CreateSpace Paperback Edition February 2013

ISBN–13: 978–0615751443
ISBN: 061575144X
Library of Congress Control Number: 2013900967

10 9 8 7 6 5 4 3 2 1

For Celina

Live a good life. If there are gods and they are just, then they will not care how devout you have been, but will welcome you based on the virtues you have lived by. If there are gods, but unjust, then you should not want to worship them. If there are no gods, then you will be gone, but will have lived a noble life that will live on in the memories of your loved ones.

—Unknown, misattributed to Marcus Aurelius

BELIEFS

Have you ever in your head,
    had the biggest ever thought?
So boggling to your mind,
    that it makes you feel distraught?

        Maybe lying in your bed,
            trying hard to fall asleep?
        You can't help but try to find,
            how and why to questions deep.

Such as, from where do we come?
    And where do we go?
What lies beyond the Universe?
    Does anybody know?

        Are you perhaps the only one,
            reflecting on such themes?
        You try to make the thoughts disperse.
            Are you as different as it seems?

Thinking as you do is common,
   many answers are conceived.
'Cause no one knows the final truth,
   these answers need to be believed.

       These things have been much dwelled upon,
          throughout our history and years.
       Really since a Stone Age youth,
          was overwhelmed by fears.

Some people try to gather views,
   maybe publish them in word.
Then to these, their own beliefs,
   they other people herd.

       They could try to reach to you,
          to get you to believe.
       What they to their great relief,
          have managed to perceive.

You may think that people have a choice,
   in what to lay their trust.
If in anything at all,
   put their faith they must.

      People don't have say or voice.
        No—not by far.
      As much as being short or tall,
        it has to do with who you are.

Children believe what their parents believe,
   and their parents they did the same.
It's very very rare,
   that held beliefs do change.

      But when it comes—that deep dark eve,
        'neath the heavens and the stars—
      skywards way you lay your stare,
        and thoughts go past the planet Mars.

Most people in our world
   belong to one of few.
Maybe Christian, Muslim, Hindu,
   Buddhist, Sikh or Jew.

Religion is the common name,
   for all of these and more.
Wherever in the world you go,
   it's hard to them ignore.

They give you answers that you seek,
   they tell you what life is.
Most say there is an afterlife.
   All try to give you bliss.

They explain the way the world was made,
   and maybe how it ends.
For some they are a perfect means,
   to make some faithful friends.

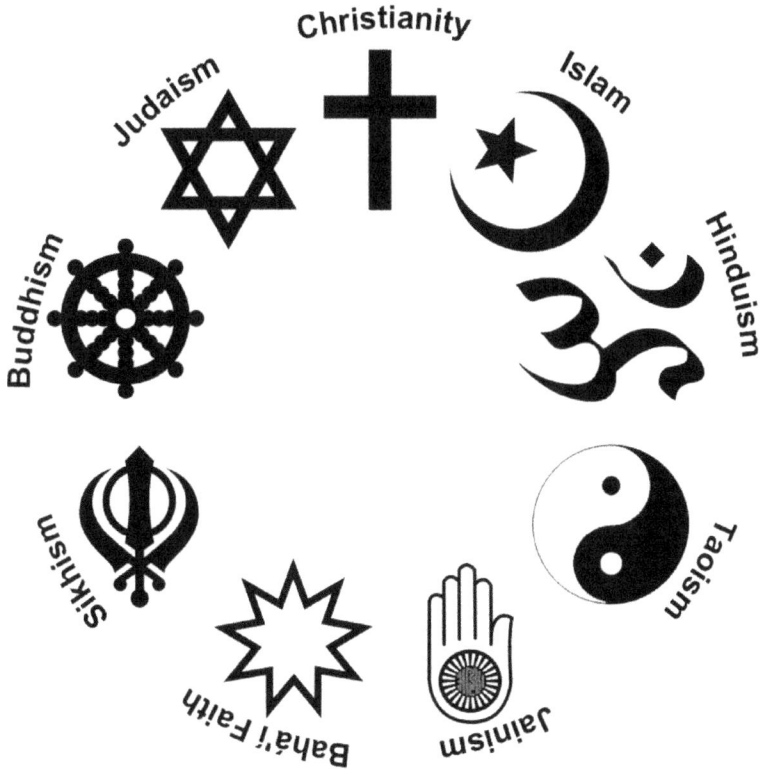

Christianity
Judaism
Islam
Buddhism
Hinduism
Sikhism
Taoism
Bahá'í Faith
Jainism

Judaism is not that big,
   but has spawned a whole lot more.
The Tanakh, Torah, Talmud,
   are texts that they explore.

A special place for this exploring,
   the Jewish house of prayer,
is the Synagogue they go to,
   a place that all Jews share.

One particular Jew named Jesus,
   two thousand years ago,
had some specific words and teachings
   that the whole world ought to know.

Thought of as the Son of God,
   he Christ was given name.
Thus giving this new religious faith,
   the name that brought it fame.

Though really only one,
    confusing as it may be,
Jesus and the Holy Ghost,
    together with God makes three.

                Jesus preached of man's acceptance,
                    of every fellow man.
                He believed in loving and forgiveness.
                    This brought him many a fan.

He himself was not accepted,
    and Christ for mankind died.
Adding his story to the Torah,
    Christians the Bible made as guide.

                Sunday is the holy day,
                    the day you go to Church.
                To hear a pastor's knowing words,
                    or one's own soul go search.

Christianity's the biggest faith,
   with Islam nigh behind.
Together these two faiths comprise
   more than half mankind.

         Islam's Muslims also share
            belief in that same Deity.
         Though they do not at all care
            for the Christian Holy Trinity.

Muhammad is the Muslim prophet,
   he himself a mortal man.
With help from angel Gabriel,
   God's words emerged as the Koran.

         The mosque is the place of worship,
            for Muslims in each state.
         Kneeling down and facing Mecca,
            they tell their God he's great.

The eastern faith of Hinduism
   is with the western ones at odds.
The biggest difference might well be,
   that they have many gods.

      Vishnu, Krishna, Shiva and Rama,
         these are only four.
      Take a look in any book:
         there are many many more.

The Vedas, or the Vedic books,
   are ancient Indian scripts.
As the foundation of their faith,
   Hindus must with them come to grips.

      The Temple is the place they go,
         to bring an offer sweet.
      It also represents the place,
         where gods and mankind meet.

A relatively modern faith
　　is also found out east.
A difference from other ones
　　is that Sikhism doesn't have priests.

　　　　Baptized Sikhs must take good care
　　　　　that they always have a place,
　　　　for things that they are bound to wear,
　　　　　on their person, called five Ks.

A Sikh's a holy soldier,
　　defender of things dear.
Faith and justice for one and all,
　　this is very clear.

　　　　Guru Granth Sahib
　　　　　is their written creed.
　　　　It's what all Sikhs read,
　　　　　when they guidance need.

Buddhism too,
   is an eastern belief—
one that in the figure Buddha
   has a popular motif.

      Buddha was a man,
         who became enlightened—
      which means that his senses
         were all much heightened.

Having no gods,
   but a belief that a human mind,
with reason can end suffering,
   and open the eyes of blind.

      Of karma and rebirth,
         you might already have heard.
      You do not have to read,
         the Tipitaka's every word.

These were some.
   There are many many more.
But I'll leave it up to you,
   to open up that door.

            Religions are plenty,
               but are they always good?
            That there are problems with religion
               should be understood.

Now's not the time to be naive.
   Let's try not to be ideal.
Much of the world's despair
   is brought about by religious zeal.

            Religion is, to many folks,
               the only path to choose.
            However, many people,
               all beliefs refuse.

People in this category,
   number quite a few.
They believe that every faith,
   tells many things untrue.

      They instead rely on reason,
        in science and on mind.
      Through rational mentation,
        worldly proofs they try to find.

Atheist, Humanist, Agnostic,
   Freethinker, Nontheist,
are names you might call people,
   who in non-belief persist.

      Secular ideologies
        see meaning in this life.
      Intrinsic moral ethics
        clear up all laic strife.

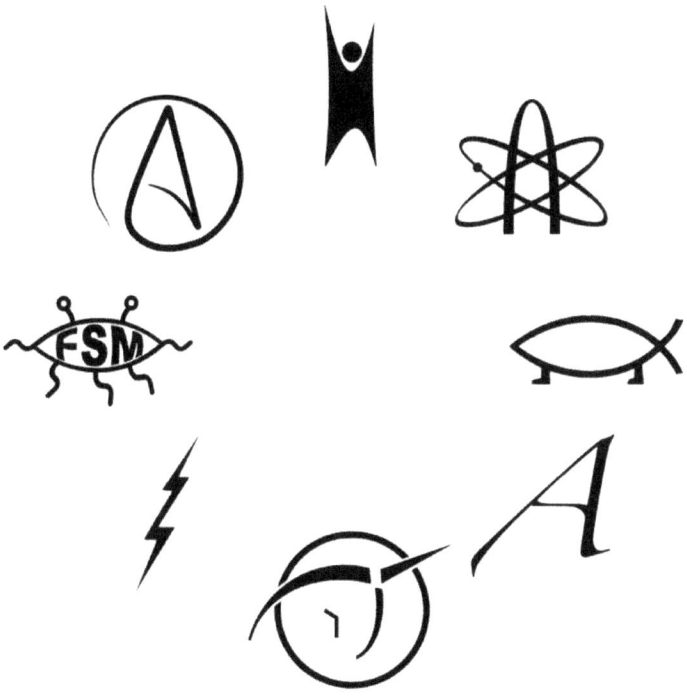

Now, the lesson to receive
    is that you have a choice—
to believe or not believe—
    in that you should rejoice.

We are all equipped,
    with a most wonderful tool—
        a kind of built in lens.

            Far from a script,
                it imaginations fuel—
                    it's called your common sense!

Own Meditations

Own Contemplations

Own Speculations

Own Deliberations

Own Ruminations

Coming soon to an Amazon page near you

Change: A Children's Guide to Evolution
by Sven O Mag

Much more than you'd think,
or more than you're told,
the world is indeed
horrendously old.

Recommended Reading

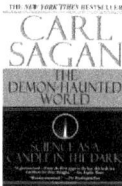

The Demon-Haunted World
by Carl Sagan

How can we make intelligent decisions about our lives
if we don't understand the difference between myths
and the testable hypotheses of science? Scientific
thinking is critical to the pursuit of truth.

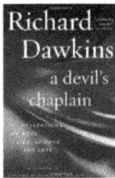

A Devil's Chaplain
by Richard Dawkins

Dawkins weighs in on topics as diverse as ape rights,
jury trials, religion, and education, all examined
through the lens of natural selection and evolution.

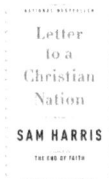

Letter to a Christian Nation
by Sam Harris

Sam Harris tries to bring enlightenment to a nation
regressing more and more into ignorance.

Life of Pi
by Yann Martel

Life of Pi is a beautiful story about survival and
religion. During a move of his family's zoo, Pi is
shipwrecked in the Pacific Ocean together with a few
of the zoo's animals.

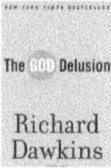

The God Delusion
by Richard Dawkins

A preeminent scientist, and the world's most prominent atheist, asserts the irrationality of belief in God and the grievous harm religion has inflicted on society, from the Crusades to 9/11.

God is not Great
by Christopher Hitchens

Hitchens, one of our great political pugilists, makes the ultimate case against religion. He frames the argument for a more secular life based on science and reason.

The End of Faith
by Sam Harris

In The End of Faith, Sam Harris tells why religious fundamentalism may appear harmless, but also why they're not—they are in fact very dangerous and threaten all of mankind.

Breaking the Spell
by Daniel C. Dennett

Religion examined scientifically. Is religion a product of blind evolutionary instinct or rational choice? Is it truly the best way to live a moral life?

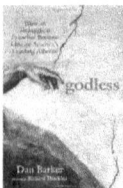

Godless
by Dan Barker

The co-president of the Freedom From Religion Foundation documents his journey from being an evangelical minister to coming out as an atheist.

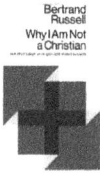

Why I Am Not a Christian …
by Bertrand Russell

Essays on religion and related subjects. Russell's reasoned opposition to any system or dogma, which he feels may shackle man's mind, runs through all the essays in this book.

Science and Religion
by Daniel C. Dennett and Alvin Plantinga

An enlightening debate that will motivate students to think critically—is Christianity compatible with evolutionary theory?

Why People Believe Weird Things
by Michael Shermer

Shermer debunks popular superstitions and prejudices and explores the very human reasons people find otherworldly phenomena, conspiracy theories, and cults so appealing.

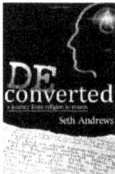

Deconverted
by Seth Andrews

Former religious radio host, Seth Andrews, attempts to reconcile faith and the facts led him to a conclusion previously unthinkable.

Critical Thinking in Psychology: Separating Sense from Nonsense
by John Ruscio

The author differentiates science and pseudoscience, and teaches the fundamentals of scientific reasoning.

The God Virus
by Darrel W. Ray

This book will give you the tools to understand religion and its power in you, your family and your culture.

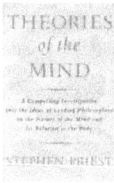

Theories of the Mind
by Stephen Priest

Readers are walked through the main schools of philosophical thought, and are offered a compelling new solution to the great philosophical puzzle of the relationship between the body and the mind.

The Problems of Philosophy
by Bertrand Russell

This classic work, first published in 1912, has never been supplanted as an approachable introduction to the theory of philosophical inquiry.

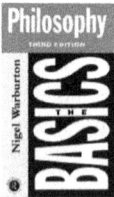

Philosophy: The Basics
by Nigel Warburton

Can you prove God exists? How do we know right from wrong? These are just two of many philosophical questions addresses in this book.

The Moral Landscape
by Sam Harris

Defining morality in terms of human and animal well-being, Harris argues that science can do more than tell how we are; it can, in principle, tell us how we ought to be.

The Elegant Universe
by Brian Greene

Pulitzer Prize finalist Brian Greene peels away the layers of mystery surrounding string theory to reveal a universe that consists of 11 dimensions where the fabric of space tears and repairs itself.

Unweaving the Rainbow
by Richard Dawkins

Dawkins takes up the most important and compelling topics in modern science. Mysteries don't lose their poetry because they are solved: the solution often is more beautiful than the puzzle.

The Dragons of Eden
by Carl Sagan

Sagan offers his vivid and startling insight into the brain of man and beast, the origin of human intelligence, the function of our most haunting legends, and their amazing links to recent discoveries.

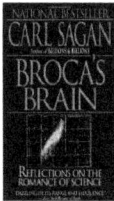

Broca's Brain
by Carl Sagan

Sagan explores and explains a mind-boggling future of intelligent robots, extraterrestrial life and its consequences, and other provocative, fascinating quandaries of the future that we want to see today.

Intelligent Thought
by John Brockman

Essays by fifteen preeminent thinkers reveal the fact and power of evolution, and the beauty of the scientific quest to understand our world.

www.ingramcontent.com/pod-product-compliance
Lightning Source LLC
Chambersburg PA
CBHW060629030426
42337CB00018B/3271